The Little
Book of
MOTHER
TERESA

The Little
Book of
MOTHER
TERESA

SANGEET DUCHANE

FALL
RIVER
PRESS

Design by NightwindCreative.com
Cover by Bullet Liongson

Fall River Press
122 Fifth Avenue
New York, NY 10011

ISBN: 978-0-7607-5450-4

Printed and bound in Singapore

3 5 7 9 10 8 6 4

CONTENTS

Early Life

The woman who would later become the famous Mother Teresa was born as Agnes Bojaxhiu on August 26, 1910 in the city of Skopje in what is now the Republic of Macedonia. Some biographers say that her middle name was

Gonxha (flowerbud) and others that this was a nickname she was given later in childhood. In either event, she became known as Agnes Gonxha Bojaxhiu.

Her parents were Nikola and Dranafile Bojaxhiu, and Nikola was a merchant from a prosperous merchant family. Agnes had an older brother and sister named Lazar and Aga. Both Nikola and Drana, as she was called, considered themselves ethnic Albanians, though they came from a part of Yugoslavia that was once part of Serbia. Today the governments of Albania and Macedonia, where Skopje is now located, are arguing over who gets to claim Mother Teresa.

The city of Skopje has had a long and varied history, and at the time of Agnes's birth it was part of the Ottoman Empire. It had been established in antiquity as an Illyrian city that became a Roman post called Scupi in the fourth century C.E. In 1189 it was conquered by the Serbs and in 1392 by the Ottoman Turks. It remained part of the Ottoman Empire until 1913, when it was again conquered by the Serbs.

The transition from Turkish to Serbian rule was not an easy one, and the unrest had a major impact on Agnes's life. Ethnic Albanians in the area complained of atrocities by the Serbs and petitioned the League of Nations to let them join Albania. Nikola Bojaxhiu was a supporter of Albanian independence and attended a gathering in support of independence for ethnic Albanians in Belgrade in 1918. He returned home with internal hemorrhaging and died after emergency surgery. Lazar Bojaxhiu always believed that his father was poisoned.

Nikola's business partners quickly took his assets, leaving Drana and the children with little more than the house they lived in. Agnes, at 8, went from being the child of prosperity to a child living on the edge of poverty. Drana rallied herself from her grief and began to support the family with sewing, embroidery, and trading in cloth.

Before his death, Nikola had been a strong advocate for charity. His children remember him as saying, "My child, never eat a single mouthful unless you are sharing with others." His young wife Drana continued this charity after he was gone.

Though she and the children had little, there was usually some-one there to share it. Agnes would realize as she got older that not all the people in the house were relatives as she had believed as a small child. Some were people from the community that her mother had taken in. Agnes's mother's advice on charity also impressed her. Drana said, "When you do good, do it quietly, as if you were throwing a stone in the sea."

The Bojaxhiu family was Roman Catholic, part of a small minor-ity in that predominantly Islamic edge of the Turkish Empire. Of the Christians in the area, most were Orthodox, not Roman Catholic. As a small minority, the Catholics were tight-knit and fiercely protective of their faith. When Nikola was head of the household, political con-cerns were often discussed, but when the more religious Drana assumed that role, religion became much more of a focus.

Agnes was influenced by a Croatian Jesuit named Father Jambrekovic, who taught her the spiritual exercises of the Jesuit founder, Ignatius Loyola: "What have I done for Christ? What am I doing for Christ? What will I do for Christ?" He told her about Jesuit Yugoslavian missionary work in India and gave her copies of a magazine called *Catholic Missions*. She read there of nuns who lived in huts in wild areas and confronted tigers and other wild animals. They and the villagers were often on the edge of starvation. As a young child Agnes had been interested in missionary work in Africa, but now she began to turn her sights toward India.

Agnes was active in Church activities as a girl, belonging to a youth group and singing in the choir, where both she and Aga were frequent soloists. By age 12, she began to think she had a vocation, or call to be a nun, but she was not sure. She asked Father Jambrekovic how she would know, and he told her that the proof of the right in any endeavor is joy. If she felt joy, that was the compass pointing toward her true direction in life.

Her brother Lazar tells stories about her during this time that reveal her to be both devout and a stickler for rules. At that time Roman Catholics could not take communion unless they had fasted from the midnight before. Lazar, being a fairly typical boy, would sometimes sneak into the kitchen for a snack after midnight. If she caught him, Agnes would give him a lecture on fasting before communion, but she never told their mother about the late-night raids. Lazar also remembered a priest named Father Zadrima, who enforced a strict discipline with the aid of a thick walking stick. When Lazar expressed his dislike of this priest, he remembered that Agnes told him, "It is your duty to love him and give him respect. He is Christ's priest."

Agnes was not a healthy child, suffering from malaria, a club foot, and a tendency toward respiratory infections. Each year many people in the community, including non-Catholics, joined a pilgrimage to the shrine of the Madonnna of Letnice on the slopes of Skopje's Black Mountain. Drana used to arrange for Agnes to spend extra time there because of her poor health. It was there that Agnes prayed about her future and finally decided, at age 18, that she had a religious vocation.

When she first heard the news, Drana was not overjoyed. A vocation would take her daughter away from the close-knit family. Drana refused permission and shut herself in her room for 24 hours. When she came out again she had reconciled herself, and told Agnes that she would give her permission if Agnes would promise her to be, "only, all for God and Jesus." This would be a frequent refrain in Agnes's later life, and something she would tell her sisters when she founded an order.

Agnes had decided to join the Loreto Sisters, the Irish branch of the Institute of the Blessed Virgin Mary, whose work

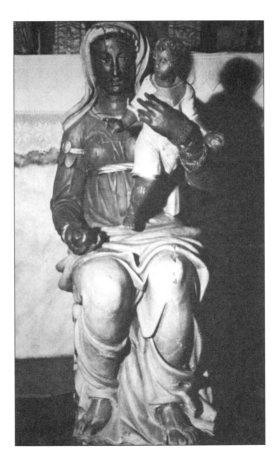

had been praised by Yugoslavian priests in Bengal. The Loreto Sisters were dedicated to providing an education for girls. Because Nikola had been progressive in his belief that his daughters as well as his son should receive educations, Agnes was prepared to train as a teacher.

It is easy to love the people far away.

It is not always easy to love those close to us.

It is easier to give a cup of rice to relieve

hunger than to relieve the loneliness and pain

of someone unloved in our own home.

Bring love into your home, for this is where

our love for each other must start.

A New Life

gnes traveled to Paris with another girl from her area who had also decided to join the Loreto Sisters. After being accepted in Paris, they were sent on to Dublin for a short training period, and then sent by ship to India. On the ship they joined sisters from other missionary orders who were also making the journey. Now it was Agnes's turn to write letters to *Catholic Missions,* and when she first saw Madras, she wrote of her shock in what she found there:

> Many families live in the streets, along the city walls, even in places thronged with people. Day and night they live out in the open on mats they have made from large palm leaves—or frequently on the bare ground. They are all virtually naked, wearing at best a ragged loincloth.... If our people could only see

all this, they would stop grumbling about their own misfortunes and offer thanks to God for blessing them with such abundance.

Agnes and her companion went to the Loreto convent at the hill station of Darjeeling to do their novitiate. They had entered into the height of the British Raj in India, where the British effectively controlled both the wealth and the government of the land. A very status-conscious British community had a culture of its own

that overlaid, but excluded, the Indian culture of the majority. Education provided by European sisters could often be useful for Indians in learning to deal with and function within the Raj.

At Darjeeling Agnes became Sister Teresa. She wanted to take Thérèse of Lisieux, the saint known as

the Little Flower, for her patron saint, but there was already a member of the Loreto order in India named Thérèse, so she had to take the Spanish spelling of the name instead. This is the name of another saint, the 16th-century Spanish saint Teresa of Avila. Though Mother Teresa later denied any intention of taking Teresa of Avila as her patron saint, she followed Teresa's example of founding an order with more strict observances than were common in her time.

Sister Teresa and her fellow novitiates studied to be teachers, learning Hindi and Bengali, as well as other subjects. Teresa also worked briefly to help the nursing staff at a medical station in Darjeeling. She remembered a time when a man brought a boy on the point of death:

The man is afraid we will not take the child, and says, "If you do not want him, I will throw him into the grass. The jackals will not turn up their noses at him." My heart freezes. The poor child! Weak, and blind—totally blind. With much pity and love I take the little one into my arms, and fold him in my apron. The child has found a second mother.

Mother Teresa's authorized biographer, Kathryn Spink says that during her novitiate Sister Teresa was known for her deeply spiritual attitude toward suffering. "In other respects she was for the most part unremarkable, not particularly educated, not particularly intelligent. In fact it was for her ineptitude at lighting the candles for Benediction that some remember her best."

At the end of her training period in Darjeeling, Sister Teresa was sent as a teacher to Loreto Entally, one of six schools run by the Loreto order in Calcutta (now known as Kolkata) at that time. The Loreto order was known throughout India for the quality of its education. Though only 2% of the population of India was Christian, 20% were educated by Catholic teaching orders. The school where

Sister Teresa taught educated girls from wealthy Indian families and subjects were taught in English. There was another school in the same compound for poorer children where classes were held in Bengali and taught by sisters from the Daughters of St. Anne, an order of Bengali women associated with Loreto.

Sister Teresa taught geography and then history, and has been described as an inspiring teacher. The life was a quiet one, as the Loreto order was semi-cloistered, and the women could not go outside the convent walls except to go on an annual retreat to Darjeeling or for an emergency, such as a hospital visit. In such travel, a member of Loreto would be sheltered in a private car and accompanied by another member of the order.

Another sister at Loreto recalls Teresa during this period as someone very much in love with God, friendly, but not distracted by friendship from her devotions.

On May 24, 1937, at the age of 26, Sister Teresa took her final vows at Loreto and became Mother Teresa. All the women of the Loreto order who have taken final vows are known by the title Mother. She continued as a teacher, a role she would fill for 19 years.

Hard times were coming to Calcutta that would change Mother Teresa's life. There had always been poverty in Calcutta during the British Raj, but officials had worked to keep it on the back streets, out of sight of the British social life. With the outbreak of World War II, things changed.

As a British possession, India was automatically the enemy of the Axis powers. Floods and a cyclone in 1942 destroyed most of the crops in Bengal, so when Japanese forces occupied Burma and cut off the rice supply to Bengal in 1943, things became desperate. Famine struck and refugees poured into the city. British mismanagement and corruption in the management of the food supplies made things worse. Other British, especially the women, did what they could to help. Houses were filled with refugees and food was distributed, but millions died in spite of all efforts.

During the war many of the students were evacuated and the elderly headmistress of Entally was sent away. Mother Teresa was appointed headmistress in her absence. Her letter to her mother on that occasion, and her mother's response provide an interesting illustration of their relationship. "This is a new life. Our center here is very fine." Mother Teresa wrote, "I am a teacher, and I love the work. I am also the Head of the whole school, and everybody wishes me well." "Dear child," her mother replied, "do not forget that you went to India for the sake of the poor."

In 1942 Entally school was requisitioned for a military hospital and Mother Teresa had to oversee a move to a smaller building. At the end of the war, students and teachers returned. There was some question about Mother Teresa's suitability as a headmistress, so the job was returned to the former Head and Mother Teresa acted as her assistant.

It was soon clear that though Britain had been "victorious" in the war, it had survived as a weakened nation. It no longer had the strength or will to oppose an independent India. Negotiations began for the partition of India into two new nations: Hindustan and Pakistan. Tension between Hindus and Muslims ran high and riots broke out in Calcutta.

One day there was no food to feed the teachers and hundreds of girls at Entally, so Mother Teresa broke the enclosure rules and walked out to find food. The day she chose to do this happened to be the day of one of the worst riots in Calcutta, in which at least 5,000 people were killed. She was shocked and horrified by the gore and violence, but she found some rice and army officers escorted her back to the convent.

Love is like a fruit in season at all times.

Love can warm three winter months.

Inspiration

In 1946 Mother Teresa was ill and was sent to Darjeeling for her annual retreat and to rest and recuperate. In the train to Darjeeling on September 10—a day since celebrated as Inspiration Day by the Missionaries of Charity—Mother Teresa believed that she was called to start a new order.

The new order was to be dedicated to the Immaculate Heart of Mary and its aim was to "quench the infinite thirst of Jesus Christ on the cross for love of souls." This is based on the words of Jesus on the cross as reported in John 19:28, "I thirst." Missionary of Charity chapels around the world have that inscription.

When she returned to Calcutta from Darjeeling, Mother Teresa went to her spiritual advisor Father Van Exem, who supported her and took her request to then Archbishop Périer. The archbishop was less enthusiastic than Father Van Exem about the plan. There were already several Catholic orders working with the poor in India. Also, that was a time of strong Indian nationalism and a natural resentment of European influence. He did not feel it was safe to send a European woman into the slums alone. Another sister had made a similar request and then had thanked him profusely after he talked her out of it. He suspected that Mother Teresa would also think better of the plan.

In that he underestimated her. He ordered her to wait one year before sending her request to the Vatican. She obeyed more in form than in spirit. She did not send her request to the Vatican, but she repeatedly told Father Van Exem that Jesus wanted the foundation right away and encouraged him to return to Archbishop Périer repeatedly to ask him to change his mind, all to no avail. The Archbishop stood firm.

During this period Mother Teresa was transferred to Ansansol, about three hours from Calcutta by train. She was put in charge of the garden there and seemed to enjoy the change. It was not to last, however. About six months later Archbishop Périer directed Loreto to bring her back to Calcutta where he could watch her more closely.

In January of 1948 Archbishop Périer decided that Mother Teresa was not going to change her mind and should be allowed to make her request for a release from her order, which is called an indult. There are two kinds of indults possible. One is the indult of exclaustration, which means that the religious can leave a convent or monastery, but is still bound by religious vows. The other is the indult of secularization, which means that the religious person becomes a layperson again.

Archbishop Périer ordered that Mother Teresa demonstrate her trust in God by asking for an indult of secularization. Mother Teresa wrote a letter first to her Mother General of Loreto, asking for her permission to seek an indult of exclaustration. Archbishop Périer insisted on reviewing the letter, and then rewrote it to conform to his instructions to her. The reply from the Mother General gave permission for her to request an indult from Rome, but urged her to seek an indult of exclaustration instead of secularization.

Archbishop Périer was not to be swayed from his determination that she demonstrate her trust by asking for secularization. Perhaps he felt that was a test of her determination to make such a significant change. The letter requesting an indult of secularization was sent off to Rome via Delhi. Years later Mother Teresa would discover that the letter never reached Rome. Church officials in Delhi, very aware of the desperate need in India at that time for relief of the poor, granted her a one-year indult of exclaustration, during which time the Archbishop was to evaluate her work and decide if she could apply to found a new order.

The news of her plans caused quite a stir in Entally. There was so much distress and discussion that a notice was placed on a blackboard, "Do not criticize. Do not praise. Pray."

It was decided that Mother Teresa would be sent to Patna, to a medical center run by a different order of sisters, to learn medical skills for her new work. In preparation for her new life she went into the bazaar and bought three of the cheapest saris she could find. They were white with three blue stripes on the edges. She said that she liked the blue, because it reminded her of the Virgin Mary. She wore the saris over a plain white habit. To avoid difficult farewells, she left Entally at night, taking with her the three saris, her ticket to Patna, five rupees, and a few personal belongings.

Both Father Van Exem and Archbishop Périer were insistent that Mother Teresa receive adequate medical training. Mother Teresa's biographer Spink says that they were worried that she might cause a scandal by making a mistake. After only a few weeks, and very scanty training, Mother Teresa announced that she was ready to start her work. She may have been impatient with the training, but she may also have been anxious to use her one year to prove herself in real work. When her supervisors at Patna supported her, Father Van Exem and Archbishop Périer allowed her to return to Calcutta. She was 38 years old.

We need silence to be alone with God,

to speak to him, to listen to him, to ponder

his words deep in our hearts. We need to be

alone with God in silence to be renewed and

transformed. Silence gives us a new outlook on

life. In it we are filled with the energy of God

himself that makes us do all things with joy.

A New Venture

Mother Teresa lodged at first in a Carmelite house that followed rules of poverty similar to the ones she wanted to adopt for her new order. She traveled from there to the slums each day to do her work. She apparently started out with only a vague idea of what the work among the poorest of the poor would be. As an experienced teacher the first thing she did was to gather a group of children around her and begin to teach them the Bengali alphabet. She had no teaching supplies, so she scratched her lessons in the dirt. She also taught the children hygiene at a nearby pump and taught them the Catholic catechism, though most were not Christian.

Mother Teresa was always a popular teacher, and the slum children seemed to like her as much as her more sheltered charges at Entally had done. Large numbers of children came to her, and this popularity helped her to gain the trust of people in the slum community who might have been suspicious of a European from another religion. India, however, also has a deep respect for people from any religious tradition who have given their lives to a religious pursuit, and religious people are given honor, whatever their religion and whatever their nationality. Mother Teresa, as a religious woman, was considered worthy of respect.

Mother Teresa soon found herself confronted with the kind of medical situation her superiors had feared. She met a man with a gangrenous thumb who needed to have the thumb removed to survive. Knowing this, but lacking the training to know how to perform the procedure, Mother Teresa took a pair of scissors and cut off the thumb. Her patient fainted in one direction, and she fainted in the other.

One day she had an experience that would change the direction of her work forever. She found a woman who was dying and tried to take her to a hospital. The hospitals, however, were overflowing with patients, who lined the hallways and lobbies as well as filling the rooms. In an overcrowded area where people were weakened by a lack of food and a paucity of medical care, disease was raging through the poorer population. The hospitals, as a matter of policy, could only take patients who had a chance of survival. They could not provide space for people to die.

Many people were trying to help with this situation. Various relief organizations, including both Protestant and Catholic organizations, were doing what they could, but the situation was out of control. There were two million refugees in the city, and though the government set up medical dispensaries and soup kitchens, they were unable to meet all the needs of the poor. Departing British officials had left the untrained and inexperienced Indian officials with an unmanageable situation. As the rest of the world recovered from the effects of war, India was left to deal with much of the problem on its own.

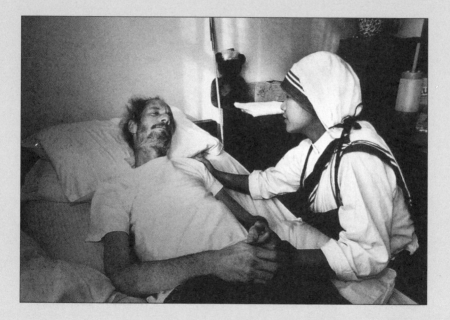

Kind words can be short and easy to speak,

but their echoes are truly endless.

The Order

By this time some of Mother Teresa's former students were anxious to join her. She spent a great deal of time trying to find a space where she and other women could live together until the Church decided whether it would approve the new order. A Catholic man, Michael Gomes, finally offered the upper two floors of his house, once they were repaired. Two of his brothers had gone to Pakistan to help Christians there, so the space was unused. Mr. Gomes and his family lived on the first floor, which would provide a certain amount of protection and privacy for the women living above.

At first Mother Teresa moved in alone, while the upper floor was still being prepared. She would work in the slums until about five or six in the evening, and then return to the Gomes home to devote herself to prayer and writing. One of the tenets of the new order was that they were to rely on Divine Providence for their support and the support of their work. Mother Teresa supported herself and her work by begging, though she did not always get enough to allow her to eat. She would write notes to Mr. Gomes, "Mr. Gomes, I have nothing to eat. Please give me something to eat."

Once space was available, one of Mother Teresa's former students joined her. She took the religious name of Sister Agnes, because Agnes had been Mother Teresa's baptismal name. Other young women soon followed. These girls joined Mother Teresa each day in the slums and also begged door to door. The people who lived in the area had very little, but were usually willing to give something to help others.

The one-year review of Mother Teresa's work was successful, and on October 7, 1950 the Order of the Missionaries of Charity was officially established, with Mother Teresa as the head of the Order. She was now faced with the need to find a Mother House for the new order. A Muslim man was selling his home and moving to Pakistan, and the priest negotiating on behalf of Mother Teresa managed to get him to agree to sell the house for less than the land alone was worth. He did this because the house would be used for religious purposes. (Islam includes Christianity as one of the religions of the Book, and charity is one of the five pillars of Islam. Though Islam has never encouraged monasticism, a group of religious women working with the poor was something this gentleman could appreciate.)

Mother Teresa insisted that "Our rigorous poverty is our safe-guard," and said, "We do not want to do what other religious organizations have done throughout history, and begin by serving the poor only to end up by unconsciously serving the rich. In order to understand and help those who have nothing, we must live like them." She had originally intended that she and the sisters of the order would live like the poor by eating the diet of the poorest of the poor: rice and salt. While she was at the medical mission in Patna, the sisters there had talked her out of that idea. They said that enforcing such a diet would be a sin and that women could not sustain hard work on such a diet. They would simply succumb to the same diseases from which the poor community suffered. Mother Teresa bowed to their greater knowledge and agreed to a more balanced diet.

The sisters of the new order got up at 4:30 in the morning (4:15 on Sunday), dressed with a sheet over their heads, washed their faces with cold water from a tank, cleaned their teeth with ashes from the kitchen stove. They washed themselves and did their laundry with cold water from a bucket, one of their few

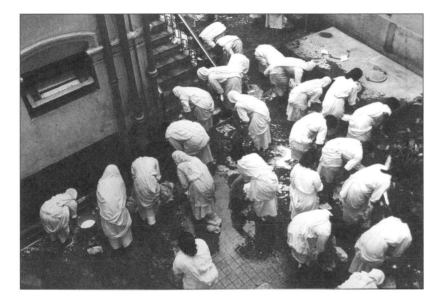

possessions. The sisters would each have a very small piece of soap that they would use to wash both themselves and their clothes.

Washing and doing laundry from a bucket was fairly common, even for the middle-class Indian of that time. For many years after, many Indian bathrooms would be a tiled or cement room with a cold tap in one wall and a floor slanting toward a drain. The family

would fill the bucket and use a scoop or small container to shower. The family laundry would often be done in that room as well. The poorest of the poor had only water tanks or pumps in public places or rivers to bathe in.

After their morning ablutions, the sisters would gather for prayer and meditation, followed by Mass.

Before eating breakfast, the sisters were required to drink a glass of water. At breakfast, they were required to drink reconstituted powdered milk and eat five chapattis with ghee (clarified butter), whether they were hungry or not, and take a vitamin pill. These eating requirements were considered part of the discipline.

By 7:45 they went out to work among the poor and returned to the Mother House at noon for the midday break. They said prayers and then had a lunch that consisted of five ladles of bulgur wheat and three bits of meat, if meat was available.

Lunch was followed by housework and half an hour of rest. They then gathered for a tea of two dry chapattis, followed by half an hour of spiritual reading or instruction by Mother Teresa. The majority of the sisters at this time were young Indian women, not all from Christian homes, who got the majority of their religious training from Mother Teresa and the priests she brought in to instruct them.

After this instruction, the sisters went out for an additional three or four hours of work, returning to the Mother House at six in the evening. They gathered for prayer and adoration of the sacrament, followed by a dinner of rice and dhal and vegetables, which was accompanied by ten minutes of spiritual reading.

During the entire day, the sisters did not speak to each other or to anyone else about anything but essential business. As they walked in the streets, they said their rosaries. In fact, this upset some people who felt ignored by the sisters, and Mother Teresa had to remind them to pay attention to others and be friendly at the same time they continued to say the rosary. The only time that the sisters were released from this requirement was the time between the end of dinner and bed at ten. This was the time set aside for mending their clothing and sheets and for recreation.

In the beginning things were difficult, since the order was not well enough known to always receive enough support. When there was no fuel to cook food, they ate raw wheat, sometimes soaked overnight. In spite of these hardships, and perhaps because of them, the group was cohesive and met these challenges as new adventures.

On Sundays the sisters walked long distances collecting children to take to Sunday school and Mass. On Thursdays they had a day of rest from any work outside the house, and Archbishop Périer often insisted that Mother Teresa take the young women to a doctor's garden for a picnic.

Though Mother Teresa wanted her order to live like the poorest of the poor, she was equally clear that she did not want them to live among the poorest of the poor. This would later create philosophical differences with other groups of relief workers. In Mother Teresa's view, the most important thing for the sisters was the fact that they were sisters. Being religious women had to be the focus of their lives. It was essential for them to retreat at the end of each day to a place where they could pray and meditate, before setting off to work again the next day.

Mother Teresa insisted that the sisters speak only English among themselves, even though most of them were Indian and some did not speak English. The reason she said was that a common language was needed, and most of the religious material they had available was in English. In the early days Mother Teresa found time to tutor some of the young women who had left Entally without finishing their studies for their final exams, and sent one woman to study to be a doctor.

Though Mother Teresa was very clearly the head of this order and freely exercised her authority, she joined the sisters in hard work and never avoided even the most menial of tasks, such as cleaning the bathroom. She stayed up later than the sisters each night to work, and though there was something of a competition among the sisters to beat her to the chapel in the morning, few ever succeeded.

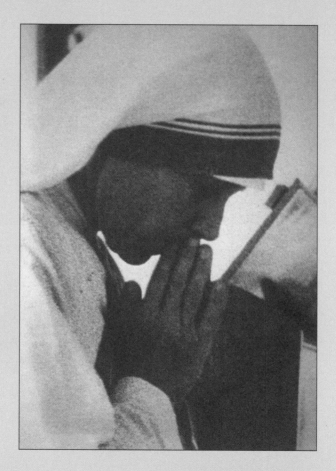

We need to find God, and he cannot be found

in noise and restlessness. God is the friend of

silence. See how nature—trees, flowers, grass

—grows in silence; see the stars, the moon

and the sun, how they move in silence...

We need silence to be able to touch souls.

Work in Calcutta

Once young women began to join her, Mother Teresa was ready to do the work she had identified as needed in the poorest communities. She had noticed earlier that the terminally ill poor had no place to go. In 1952 the situation became a public issue. Calcutta residents saw a boy lying in the gutter and called an ambulance to take him to the hospital. When he was taken to the hospital, he was refused entry as a hopeless case, and the ambulance returned him to the gutter, where he died. The residents were outraged and created a scandal in the press.

Mother Teresa, always good at taking offered opportunities, went to the city governments and told them that she and her sisters would provide care for the dying if the city would give them a space to use. She would provide care only for the people that the hospitals would not take. The city agreed to have her help with what was clearly a serious problem, and gave the Missionaries of Charity two rooms in a building called the Kalighat. This was a combination temple to the Goddess Kali and a burning ghat, where bodies were burned for Hindus whose families could afford the wood. Cremation is the traditional death ritual in Hindu culture.

Mother Teresa and the other members of the Missionaries of Charity went out into the slums to find people who they thought were dying and brought them back to the Kalighat. The sisters sometimes had to transport them in a wheelbarrow, and the trip was probably fairly painful for many. In the center, which was named Nirmal Hriday, "Place of the Immaculate Heart," after the Immaculate Heart of Mary, the patients would be washed and given a mat or cot to lie on. They received some medical care, such as the removal of maggots from wounds, and food. Mother Teresa told the sisters to treat the body of each person as the body of Christ.

The City of Calcutta's decision to allow Catholic sisters to work out of a Hindu temple was controversial. Many people thought that it was inappropriate to have a Catholic center in a Kali temple, and some were concerned that the sisters would try to convert people to Catholicism while they were in a weakened state approaching death. Mother Teresa insisted that they only believed in conversion through love, not coercion. That was apparently not very reassuring to many people and the controversy continued. Some people went so far as to throw stones at

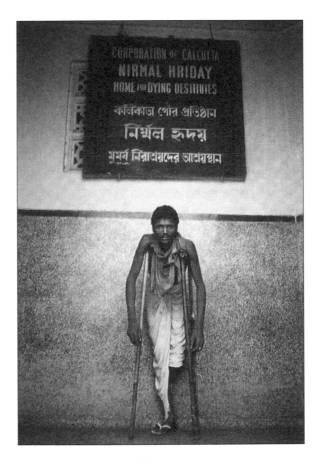

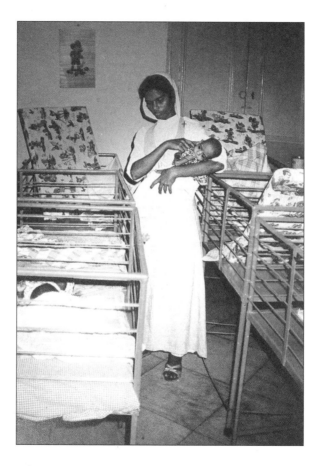

the sisters as they brought people to the temple. The protestors calmed down considerably after Mother Teresa found one of the priests from a neighboring temple collapsed in the street. Reports differ; some say he had cholera and some say tuberculosis. There were concerns about contagion and others did not want to touch him. He was cared for at Nirmal Hriday until he died.

The next big Missionaries of Charity project was to open the first Shishu Bhavan or children's home. The first was opened on September 23, 1955 with the support and assistance of Dr. B.C. Roy, a physician who was for many years the Chief Minister of West Bengal. The home accepted children of all ages.

The sick were treated and the older children were given some form of education or job training. For example, the older girls were taught to type. Eventually, the program grew and they began to send the children to school. India does not have a system of free public education, so children who attend school have to pay school fees. Mother Teresa set up a program where people could sponsor children by paying their fees. This program became so popular that by 1975 it was no longer possible to keep sponsors individually

informed about the progress of their sponsored child, and contributions were made to a World Child Welfare Fund instead.

As the children grew and prepared to leave, the sisters would arrange marriages for those who desired it, playing the part of parents in traditional Indian society. Weddings would be followed by simple receptions at the Shishu Bhavan.

The children's homes played a part in Mother Teresa's active campaign against abortion. She tried to get as much publicity as possible to let people know that if they did not want children or could not afford them the Shishu Bhavan would take them.

At one point relations were somewhat strained between Mother Teresa and the Prime Minister Indira Gandhi. Gandhi was concerned about overpopulation and the resulting problems of over-crowding, pollution, and disease epidemics. Because medical care was inadequate in many parts of India and many of the people were illiterate and unable to follow the instructions for using other forms of birth control, Gandhi's government had instituted a program of voluntary sterilization for those who already had children.

Because Catholic doctrine opposes birth control as well as abortion, Mother Teresa opposed the sterilization program and tried to talk Indira Gandhi out of it. She failed to do that, but she said in some of her public appearances that she encouraged the women of Calcutta to have all the children they wanted. Mother Teresa also had some of her workers trained in the Church-approved birth control system involving counting days from ovulation, often called the rhythm method. She had them teach it to the women they worked with. The women were given a string of beads to help them calculate the day, since many could not count. The workers tell one story that illustrates how difficult it was to teach such a complicated system. One woman came into the center pregnant and very upset. She said, "I don't understand what happened. I put the beads you gave me on the statue of Kali and still I am pregnant again!"

Next, the Missionaries of Charity tackled the problem of leprosy. Leprosy was a disease surrounded by fear and a lot of misunderstanding. It was less contagious than people believed and many forms were treatable. The damage to feet and hands and the loss of tissue was the result of injuries that occur after feeling is lost in the extremities. Because of all the fear surrounding the disease, people who had it were outcasts, even if they came from fairly well-off families.

The Missionaries of Charity set up a leper colony on the outskirts of the city, but they did not own the land and the city wanted to use it to build much-needed housing. The order started

a fundraising campaign with the slogan, "Touch a leper with your compassion." When an ambulance was donated, they started a mobile leper clinic for those who were displaced from the leper colony. They were eventually able to set up a permanent dispensary in 1959 that started out with 1,136 patients, only a small part of the 30,000 known lepers in Calcutta.

The lepers were taught to make shoes from foam rubber cuttings and old rubber tires that could protect their feet from injury. They were also taught to weave, and many wove their own bandages and made their clothing.

By 1964 the Indian government donated 34 acres of land for a leper settlement called Shanti Nagar, "the place of peace." In that year Pope Paul VI visited India and was provided with a Lincoln Continental to use during his visit. When he left, he gave the car to Mother Teresa to use in her work. The timing was perfect. She raffled the car and used the money to fund the new settlement.

The goal of the settlement was to make the residents self-sufficient. Fish ponds were built and banana and palm trees were planted to provide food. The community also raised cattle, grew rice, and tilled fields. They ran their own grocery, made baskets,

and built their own huts. The Leper colonies later took up commercial weaving as well.

Resources were always short for this project, particularly the need for surgical skills necessary to amputate gangrenous flesh. Eventually, prostheses would also be provided for amputees.

In her usual uncompromising fashion, Mother Teresa raised some controversy on the question of birth control or sterilization of women suffering from leprosy who often passed the disease on to their children. Mother Teresa was adamantly opposed to restricting those women from having children, saying that their children gave them joy.

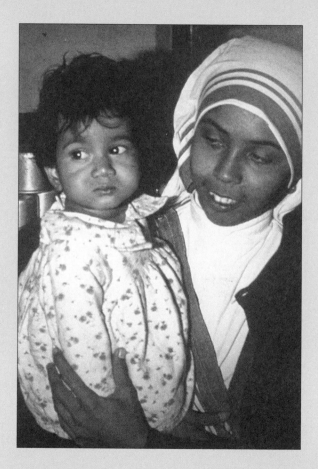

There is so much love in us all, but often we are too shy to express our love, and keep it bottled up inside us. We must learn to love, to love until it hurts, and we will know how to accept love.

Beyond Calcutta

T he Church rule for new orders is that they cannot establish houses outside the original dioceses for ten years. In the case of the Missionaries of Charity an exception was made so that they could found new houses in nine years. They were invited to establish houses in other areas of India, including Ranchi, Bombay (now Mumbai), Delhi, and Shansi.

In Delhi the order set up a new children's home, and in Bombay they found slums even worse than Calcutta and set up a home for the dying.

In 1960 Mother Teresa went to Rome to ask Pope John XXIII for special recognition for the Missionaries of Charity. She was also reunited with her brother Lazar, whom she had not seen since 1924. When she went to her audience with the pope, she lost her nerve and did not ask for his recognition of the order. She only asked for his blessing. Cardinal Agaginian of the Sacred Congregation of the Faith obtained the papal recognition for her. This meant that the congregation had papal approval and no changes to the constitutions of the order could be made without papal consent.

The work continued to expand in India. Tuberculosis clinics, pre-natal clinics, dispensaries, mobile leprosy clinics, homeless shelters, and houses for the dying were established. The sisters also set up nursery classes, primary and secondary schools, commercial and trade schools, feeding programs, and disaster aid programs. Because of the smallness of the order, the size of these programs was limited, but the sisters did what they could. When a cyclone hit Andhra Pradesh in 1977, resulting in extensive flooding and the loss of thousands of lives, ten Missionaries of Charity sisters joined the Red Cross, Christian Aid, and other charities in relief work.

You can do what I can't do.

I can do what you can't do.

Together we can do something beautiful for God.

Beyond India

In 1965 the Missionaries of Charity were invited to establish the first house outside of India, in Venezuela. The situation there was grave, as there was a serious shortage of priests and nuns to minister to the large Roman Catholic population. Mother Teresa was worried that the young order was not yet ready to be so spread out. She was afraid the spirit of the order would die out if it was spread too thin.

Archbishop Knox, the papal Internuncio to New Delhi met with her in Rome and told her that she must look at the needs of the Church before she considered the needs of her order. Mother Teresa obeyed and agreed to set up the house in Venezuela. This was a decision that would deeply affect not only the work of the Missionaries of Charity, but the life and work of Mother Teresa herself. The new house was set up on a deserted rectory in Cocorote, Venezuela. The sisters taught sewing, typing, and English, and visited the sick.

This was only the beginning of the spread of the order, and within a few years of the establishment of the first house outside

of India, Mother Teresa began to spend more and more of her time traveling around to various houses around the world and to trouble spots where houses might be established. She left Sister Agnes in charge in Calcutta and told the sisters to see God in their superiors, and told the superiors to serve and not to be served. By 1970 Mother Teresa had divided the Missionaries of Charity houses in India into five regions with regional superiors. She was then free of the day-to-day administration of the order in India, and could focus on international issues instead.

The next invitation was to set up a house in Rome to minister to the poor there. This invitation was considered a great honor, since there were already 22,000 nuns in Rome from 1,200 different orders. Mother Teresa eventually found a house for the order in a poor section of the city. Her biographers say she was delighted because it was probably the poorest Missionaries of Charity house she had found yet. The sisters worked mostly with refugees from Sicily and Sardinia.

After the house in Rome was established requests poured in from all over the world. Houses were set up in Africa, the Middle East, Latin and South America, Eastern and Western Europe, Great Britain and Ireland, Australia, Nepal, Haiti, Puerto Rico, Sri Lanka, Papua New Guinea, Australia, Japan, and the United States. The sisters worked with the poor, the homeless, AIDS patients, and refugees from natural disaster and war.

The order remained relatively small, and these houses had only a few sisters each. When someone pointed out to Mother Teresa that the efforts of the Missionaries of Charity were only a drop in a bucket, she said, "I don't think the way you do. I do not add up. I only subtract from the total number of poor and dying."

When Mother Teresa visited a Missionaries of Charity house in England, she said that she was struck by the spiritual poverty of the materially rich societies—poverty of the spirit, loneliness, unwanted people. Mother Teresa said that the reason people are poor is not that God made them so, but because "you and I do not share enough."

In her travels to the various Missionaries of Charity houses Mother Teresa tried to preserve the spirit of the order, the spirit she feared would be lost if the order was too disconnected. She had certain guidelines that the sisters were supposed to follow. For example, the sisters were not to spend money unnecessarily, such as on postage for personal letters. Donations were not to be used carelessly, because others had sacrificed to make them. Medical supplies and food were to be distributed before they spoiled.

In preserving the spirit of the order, Mother Teresa asked priests and others who worked with the order not to interfere in issues of poverty. For example, some priests suggested that the sisters have curtains in common room, but Mother Teresa said that the poorest of the poor did not have curtains, so the sisters would not have them either. She pointed out that the majority of the sisters came from relatively poor Indian backgrounds, and Mother Teresa felt it would be wrong for them to raise their standard of living by joining the order.

When houses were established in the more affluent West, luxuries such as carpeting and washing machines were also refused. In fact, Mother Teresa made headlines in San Francisco, by throwing carpeting and mattresses that had been given to the sisters out of the window when she came to open a new house there.

Mother Teresa insisted that the order have no fixed income. When New York's Cardinal Cooke offered to give the order $500 per month for every sister working in Harlem, Mother Teresa said to him, "Do you think, Your Eminence, that God is going to become bankrupt in New York?" She wanted the sisters to rely on Divine Providence from day to day.

Eventually, novitiates for the order were conduced in Manila and Rome. After their vows, the sisters would return to the Mother House in Calcutta, where they would be welcomed by a celebration and blessing by Mother Teresa. After the celebration Mother Teresa would give each of them her new assignment, and the new sister would leave within a few days, taking only a few personal belongings in a rough parcel. The sisters did not choose their assignments, but went wherever they were needed.

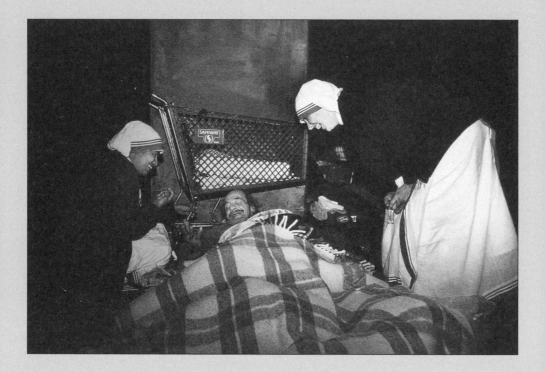

At the end of life we will not be judged by how many diplomas we have received, how much money we have made, how many great things we have done. We will be judged by, "I was hungry, and you gave me something to eat, I was naked and you clothed me. I was homeless, and you took me in." Hungry not only for bread—but hungry for love. Naked not only for clothing—but naked of human dignity and respect. Homeless not only for want of a home of bricks—but homeless because of rejection.

Letters of Mother Teresa

The work and accomplishments of Mother Teresa have been given a new perspective by the release in 2003 of letters she wrote over a period of 50 years to her spiritual directors. In those letters she expressed feelings of being abandoned by God. Some quotes follow:

I feel just that terrible pain of loss, of God not wanting me, of God not being God, of God not really existing.

I am told God lives in me, and yet the reality of darkness and coldness and emptiness is so great that nothing touches my soul.

I want God with all the power of my soul and yet between us there is terrible separation.

The damned of hell suffer eternal punishment because they experiment with the loss of God. In my own soul, I feel the terrible pain of this loss.

There is so much contradiction in my soul: such deep longing for God—so deep that it is painful, a suffering continual—and yet not wanted by God, repulsed, empty, no faith, no love, no zeal. Souls hold no attraction. Heaven means nothing; to me it looks like an empty place.

The Missionaries of Charity priest who released the letters defended his decision to make them public when Mother Teresa asked to have them destroyed, saying that the letters make Mother Teresa more human. He believes the letters make her enormous accomplishments even more remarkable, since they were done in spite of her fears and suffering.

Mother Teresa's successor as head of the Missionaries of Charity, Sister Nirmala, has said, "This is part of the spiritual life of people, and God sometimes wants to unite the soul very closely to himself. He will allow them to feel abandoned by Him. And Jesus also on the cross felt he was abandoned." Critics counter that the letters are inconsistent with the image Mother Teresa portrayed to the public.

God doesn't require us to succeed;

he only requires that you try.

Setbacks

Everything did not always go smoothly for Mother Teresa and the Missionaries of Charity. They suffered the same kinds of disappointments, setbacks, and tragedies that everyone else suffers. Mother Teresa experienced a personal disappointment when she could not get her mother and sister out of Albania, then under the repressive Hoxha regime. Mother Teresa had not seen them

since she left the family in 1924. Drana said that her last wish was to see Mother Teresa and Lazar again before she died, but the government denied Drana and Aga permission to go to Italy, where Lazar was living. This caused Mother Teresa a great deal of pain.

My mother and sister are still in Tirana. Only God knows why
they have to suffer so much. I know their sacrifices and prayers
help me in my work. It is all to the greater glory of God.

Mother Teresa thought of going to Albania to see her mother,
but she was advised that though she would surely be allowed into
the country, it was less likely that she would be let out again. For
the sake of her work, Mother Teresa decided not to go. On July 12,
1972 she got a telegram that he mother had died in Albania. Her
sister Aga died the following year, and Lazar died of cancer in 1981.

The order also had its tragedies and disappointments. The
house they had established in Belfast was closed after they felt that
the Irish did not want the order's help. Most of the sisters were
Indians and some new to Catholicism. The Irish, with their old
Catholic traditions, did not want missionaries.

In 1980 half of the 20 residents of a home for destitute women
run by the Missionaries of Charity in Kilburn, London and one vol-
unteer were killed in a fire. The fire was apparently arson, but the
accused was acquitted, and the final verdict was "Unlawful killing
by arsonist unnamed."

The sisters themselves suffered tragedies. A homeopathic doctor who did not treat herself for a dog bite died of rabies in India in 1966. In 1986, two sisters drowned trying to go through torrential rain to staff a dispensary. Mother Teresa made a memorial statement:

> The story of our two dearest Sisters who went to serve the poor and the sick, and their reward was that Jesus was very pleased with their effort so he took them to himself.... When a gardener comes to pluck the flowers, he takes the best. The same with this Jesus of ours.

Another tragedy struck close to Mother Teresa that year. She was visiting a house in Tanzania and was dropped off in a small plane. The plane tried to take off again as she and those who had come to greet her stood along the runway. The plane went out of control and plowed into the people. Three children, the manager of the leprosy center, and one sister were killed. Two children were injured.

In 1996 two Missionaries of Charity superiors died in a car crash in New York. In all these disappointments, Mother Teresa accepted the events as the will of God. She often said of people in the houses for the dying, "Today is a good day to go to Heaven."

I know God will not give me anything I can't handle.

I just wish that he didn't trust me so much.

The Brothers

The sisters of the Missionaries of Charity are most well known, but an order of brothers was established as well. A pious union of Missionaries of Charity brothers was formed under authority from the Indian bishop in 1963. Vatican permission for the establishment of an order could not happen until Mother Teresa found a man to lead it, since the Catholic Church does not allow women to head a religious congregation of men.

That problem was solved in 1963, when an Australian Jesuit, Ian Travers-Ball became interested in the new order. By then there were 12 young men in the pious union and Father Travers-Ball left the Jesuits to join them, becoming Brother Andrew. Brother Andrew revised the constitutions that Mother Teresa had written for the sisters in light of the Second Vatican Council. The brothers wore simple pants and shirts like poor people might wear around the world. A crucifix showed their religious commitment, but there was nothing else to set them apart from those around them.

At first the brothers worked with the sisters in India, but as the brothers took on projects of their own, they also began to drift apart from the sisters. Mother Teresa was adamant that the sisters were to sleep and eat in convents alone, but Brother Andrew had the brothers sleep in the same place as the people they were serving and had them eat with visitors. Both groups, however, shared the same four essentials: seriousness in prayer, love for the poor, simplicity of life, and a need for a community life.

In 1970 the brothers set up a house in the underworld of Saigon, and provided shelter and classes for 30 people. They worked there until 1975, when the new government took over the house. In 1974 Mother Teresa gave the brothers the Nivas Leprosy center at Titlagarh in which to set up a self-sufficient community. In 1975 the brothers set up another center in the skid row area of Los Angeles. They visited and assisted the old, sick, alcoholic, and alienated.

In 1978 Mother Teresa founded an additional order of contemplative brothers to complement the contemplative branch of the sisters she was forming. She did not consult Brother Andrew in

this and that caused some bad feeling, since he did not approve of seclusion from the poor. Thirteen years later, Brother Andrew said that Mother Teresa had done the right thing, though he still wished that she had communicated more with him.

Brother Andrew resigned as head of the brothers in 1986, after 21 years as the General Servant. Approximately a year later he withdrew from the order when the new head insisted that he be treated for alcoholism. Brother Andrew admitted drinking more than he should, but said he could not agree to the recommended treatment and be true to himself, and being true to himself was what he understood being a brother was about. Mother Teresa had nothing to do with the dispute.

If you judge people,

you have no time to love them.

Recognition

Worldwide recognition of Mother Teresa's work and the work of the Missionaries of Charity really began with the publication of Malcolm Muggridge's 1977 book *Something Beautiful for God*. Muggridge was a British author, lecturer, and broadcaster who had lived in Calcutta in the 1930s, during the British Raj. He remembered how the British had talked about the problems of the poor in Calcutta, but had done very little about it. He was touched and impressed by Mother Teresa's work.

Recognition inside India began a little earlier. In 1962 she had received the prestigious Padma Shri award, India's second highest honor. In 1976 she was awarded the first Pope John XXIII Peace Prize by the Vatican. An even more prestigious award for peace became hers when she was awarded the Nobel Peace Prize in 1979. The Nobel committee said:

> In the eyes of the Norwegian Nobel Committee, constructive efforts to do away with hunger and poverty, and to ensure for mankind a safer and better world community in which to develop, should be inspired by the spirit of Mother Teresa, by respect for the worth and dignity of the individual human being.

In 1983 she was awarded the Queen Elizabeth insignia of the Honorary Order of Merit, and she was later made an honorary citizen of the United States in recognition for her work.

In addition to awards, Mother Teresa was pictured with a wide variety of famous people, from Princess Diana to various U.S. Presidents. She soon got over the shyness that kept her from speaking out to the pope in 1960 and became an experienced public speaker.

The fruit of silence is prayer.

The fruit of prayer is faith.

The fruit of faith is love.

The fruit of love is service.

The fruit of service is peace.

Controversy

Perhaps inevitably, this kind of fame and acclaim also attracted controversy. This was particularly to be expected with someone as outspoken as Mother Teresa was on controversial issues. She felt that her fame should be used to publicize her views, particularly her views against abortion.

In addition to being outspoken, Mother Teresa was a very conservative Catholic. Though she bowed in obedience to the decisions of the Second Vatican Council, she never approved of priests who did not wear vestments at Mass or nuns and priests who did not wear religious clothes. (The sari and habit of the sisters of the Missionaries of Charity is considered a uniform instead of a habit.) She felt that the modern Church tended to neglect the Virgin Mary and vehemently opposed any discussion of or opposition to the decisions of the pope, including rulings on birth control and abortion.

One of her authorized biographers said of her, "In the historic struggle between Galileo and the Church, Mother Teresa would have taken the side of the Church, the side of obedient faith against radical progress based on rational evidence."

Mother Teresa differed from liberal Catholics in that she was as strongly opposed to birth control as she was to abortion, and opposed abortions in cases of rape, a risk to the mother's life, and severe deformity of the fetus. Pope John Paul II joined her in these views, and Mother Teresa took every opportunity to express them. At a Clinton Presidential Prayer Breakfast, she said, "As I am the pencil of God, I know what God likes and does not like. He does not like abortion and contraception." Her listeners were divided between outrage at her presumption in speaking for God and praise for her courage in speaking out when she knew the Clintons and many Americans disagreed with her position.

These conservative views led Mother Teresa into conflict with other women both outside and inside the Church. In 1975 she attended a Woman's Year Conference in Mexico City and advocated traditional roles for women. She believed that a woman's place is in the home and viewed the issue in terms of love:

> Love begins at home. If a woman fulfills her role in the home, if there is peace in her surroundings, there will be peace in the world. There is the part of a woman that no man can take—the

power of producing, loving others, not themselves.... The love of the unknown woman upholds the world.

Mother Teresa also adamantly opposed the women in the Catholic Church who advocated for women priests. She felt that if the Virgin Mary was not a priest, no woman should be. "Our Lady would have made the best priest, but she remained in her place." Mother Teresa upset other nuns in the United States by writing a letter to John Quinn, Archbishop of San Francisco that found its way into print. In that letter she asked him to help the Catholic nuns in the United States become more obedient to the pope.

Though there was an angry response from many nuns, a few were inspired. Five cloistered nuns in a Carmelite convent asked Mother Teresa to help them with their opposition to changes in their convent. They opposed the inclusion of television, music, newspapers, and candy.

The most public controversy was created by a British television program called *Hell's Angel,* broadcast in November 1994. This was a vitriolic criticism of Mother Teresa and her work, narrated by Washington-based British journalist Christopher Hitchens.

Hitchens criticized her position on abortion, her use of money, what he considered her personal hypocrisy, dubious medical treatment in her centers, and her friendly relationships with people like Haitian dictator "Baby Doc" Duvalier.

The program sparked widespread outrage and 200 calls, most of them critical of the program. A small group of viewers complained to the Independent Television Commission, raising issues of censorship. The Commission decided that it could not prevent criticism, no matter how popular the subject of the criticism was.

Mother Teresa asked those close to her, "Why did they do it?" Publicly she said that she forgave them. Overall the result of the program was probably more favorable to Mother Teresa than negative.

Moderate criticism the same year raised more concern. Dr. Robin Fox, writing for the prestigious medical journal *Lancet,* complained that medical care in the order's home for the dying in Calcutta was poor. He claimed that disposable needles were reused without sterilization and patients in extreme pain were given inadequate painkillers. Clifford Longley, a highly respected British lay

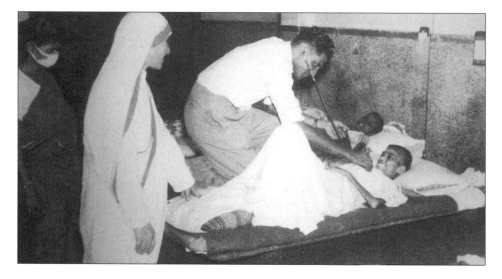

writer on religious affairs and correspondent to *The Times,* London, wrote a piece warning of the danger of a reverence for dying that turned suffering into a goal.

In 1995 an Irish paper revealed that two of the babies the Missionaries of Charity had sent for adoption from Bangladesh had gone to nonexistent families. There was concern, but many felt the good work of the order outweighed any errors.

Mother Teresa's supporters do not deny the controversies about medical care, but try to explain Mother Teresa's way of thinking. Her authorized biographer Kathryn Spink has said,

> There were those trained doctors and nurses who came to work there (Nirmal Hriday) on a voluntary basis who were horrified at the failure to observe the kind of fundamental rules of hygiene which would protect the Sisters from infection and the "patients" from contaminating each other. The Missionaries of Charity were not to wear gloves to touch the maggot-ridden bodies of the dying, any more than they were to hold the lepers at arm's length because they were tending the body of Christ.... The same kind of reasoning determined that it was not by its efficiency or effectiveness that an action should be judged but by the amount of love that was put into it.

The rules about using gloves were later changed, but the focus on love rather than merely rational concerns never did, and the controversy about levels of care continued.

Yesterday is gone.

Tomorrow is not yet come.

We have only today.

Let us begin.

Failing Health

Mother Teresa faced many health challenges in the last 14 years of her life. Her first major problem occurred earlier when she was in a car accident in 1964 and hit her head on a metal fixture on the windshield. The injury required 19 stitches, and Mother Teresa was supposed to stay in the hospital. When she discovered the cost of the care, however, she left and went to a Missionaries of Charity house to recuperate.

In 1983 she fell out of bed in the order's Rome convent and was hospitalized with an injured foot. When they examined her there, the doctors said that if she had not injured her foot and been forced to rest, she would most likely have suffered a heart attack. Mother Teresa was convinced that her guardian angel was watching over her and had pushed her out of bed so that she would get the rest and medical care she needed. During her recuperation she declined to take any pain killers, saying that she wanted to offer up her suffering to God. She was released from the hospital, but her health was fragile that year, and she had a high temperature most mornings. That did not keep her from getting up and getting to work.

By 1990 her heart trouble returned and she was hospitalized with chronic angina and malaria parasites. She was released after five weeks and told to slow down. In two weeks she was back in the hospital for a more permanent pacemaker. The next year she was hospitalized again with bacterial pneumonia. She resisted hospitalization, but finally agreed and was sent to San Diego for angioplasty to clear clogged coronary arteries after suffering heart failure brought on by pneumonia.

At this point Mother Teresa asked to resign from her position as head of the order, but when the sisters could not agree on a successor, she took up the position again.

In 1993, Mother Teresa was hospitalized again in Delhi with an attack of malaria followed by lung congestion. She was put in the coronary unit and had surgery on a closed heart vessel. She spent her 83rd birthday in the hospital. She was hospitalized again the following month for surgery to unblock another vessel.

Another fall from her bed and a broken collar bone brought Mother Teresa to the hospital in 1996, and she sprained her ankle a few months later. She was soon back in the hospital with a high

fever. Her condition was so serious that she could only breathe on a respirator, and many feared for her life. She improved, however, and insisted on being released, only to return to the hospital ten days later because of another fall. A brain scan revealed some kind of shadow on the brain, but she was released without treatment for that condition.

By the next month she was suffering from chest pains and then heart failure, and she was admitted to a special heart center in Calcutta for further surgery. At this point she insisted on resigning from her position, and the Sisters finally chose Sister Nirmala to be her successor.

During continued illness in 1997 Mother Teresa underwent an exorcism that was kept secret until 2003. Archbishop Henry D'Souza of Calcutta was hospitalized at the same time as Mother Teresa and had the same doctor. He discovered that though Mother Teresa was calm during the day, she became extremely agitated at night and pulled off wires to monitoring equipment. D'Souza believed that Mother Teresa "might be under attack of the evil one." He asked Mother Teresa if she would like an exorcism, and when she agreed, D'Souza ordered a priest in Calcutta to read a prayer of exorcism over her. The priest was uneasy, but did as he was ordered. After the procedure, the Archbishop said that Mother Teresa "slept like a baby."

D'Souza and other commentators have insisted that the exorcism does not reflect negatively on Mother Teresa's sanctity, since there was no belief that she was actually possessed by the devil, and since it is believed that holy people are often attacked by the devil, as Jesus himself was believed to be. Archbishop D'Souza said that the incident showed that Mother Teresa was both holy and human.

Mother Teresa's last public statement was on the death of Princess Diana, whom she praised for her work with the poor. On Friday, September 5, 1997, on the eve of Diana's funeral, Mother Teresa's heart finally gave out for the last time. She was laid in the Mother House in Calcutta where invited guests could view her body. She was then taken by a Missionaries of Charity ambulance to a church near the slums so that the poor could come to pay their last respects.

On September 13 her body was carried to the graveyard on the same gun carriage that was used to transport the bodies of Mahatma Gandhi and Jawaharlal Nehru. Tens of thousands lined the streets for her last farewell.

If we have no peace,

it is because we have forgotten

that we belong to each other.

Beatification

The usual procedure for evaluating a holy person for saint-hood in the Catholic Church does not begin for five years after the death of the person. In the case of Mother Teresa Pope John Paul II has waived that time period putting her on what many commentators have called the fast track to sainthood.

The procedure for naming someone a saint in the Catholic Church requires local bishops to investigate a candidate after death. A report is sent to the Vatican and reviewed by theologians and cardinals. If the person is found to be a role model for Roman Catholic virtues, the pope declares her or him Venerable. This was no problem in Mother Teresa's case.

After a candidate has been declared Venerable, one miracle has to be performed by the candidate and approved by the Vatican before the candidate can be Beatified. A 30-year-old Bengali woman, Monica Besra, has reported that she had a stomach tumor and was threatened with death. She went to the Missionaries of Charity for help and when she entered the chapel she saw a light come toward her from a picture of Mother Teresa. The sisters then prayed for her, and when she woke at 1 in the morning, the tumor was gone.

A Vatican committee approved the miracle, concluding that there was no scientific explanation for the recovery. Unfortunately, several of Besra's Indian doctors disagree. When the miracle was claimed, the West Bengal government instituted an investigation and the former West Bengal health minister, Partho De, said that he meant no disrespect to Mother Teresa, but Besra's cure was not a miracle. Doctors Manju Murshed and Ranja Mustafi, who treated Besra for tubercular meningitis, say that the tumor was related to the tuberculosis and disappeared because of extensive treatment by anti-tubercular drugs. At least one Indian doctor testified that the cure was a miracle, while Dr. Murshed claimed he was pressured by the Missionaries of Charity to change his opinion. Besra's husband also has said that her story is not true and that she was trying to get attention.

In the past Vatican committees reviewing a miracle had a devil's advocate, who argued against a miracle. A devil's advocate is no longer used and, perhaps as a result, Besra's original treating physician, who rejects the idea of a miracle, was not interviewed by the Vatican committee.

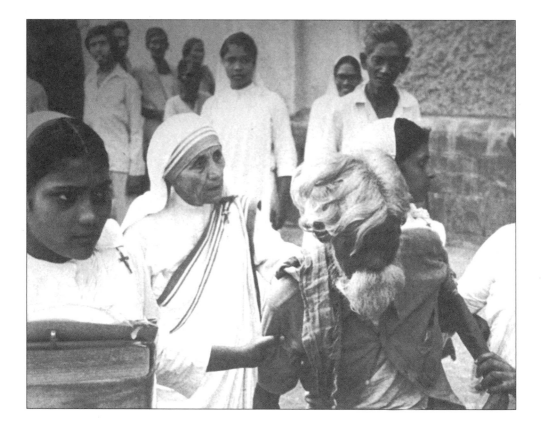

Many supporters of Mother Teresa do not care about irregularities or questions about miracles. They decided long ago that she is a saint, and welcome any validation of that opinion by the Vatican. Perhaps such a controversy in death is appropriate for a woman who so willing embraced controversy in her life. Hundreds of thousands of people turned out for her beatification ceremony in October of 2003. Thousands still gather at the anniversary of her death each year in Calcutta.

For Mother Teresa to qualify for sainthood, one more miracle must be attributed to her and approved by the Vatican.

Life is an opportunity, avail it.

Life is a beauty, admire it.

Life is bliss, taste it.

Life is a dream, realize it.

Life is a challenge, meet it.

Life is a duty, complete it.

Life is a game, play it.

Life is costly, care for it.

Life is a wealth, keep it.

Life is love, enjoy it.

Life is my story, know it.

Life is a promise, fulfill it.

Life is sorrow, overcome it.

Life is a song, sing it.

Life is a struggle, accept it.

Life is a tragedy, brace it.

Life is an adventure, dare it.

Life is life, save it!

Life is luck, make it.

*Life is too precious,
do not destroy it.*

Acknowledgements

Camera Press, 22, 44, 65, 92, 103, 106, 124; Das Studio, Darjeeling, 24; Drita Publishing, 15; Eileen Egan and the Bojaxhiu Family, 39, 40, 80, 86, 110, 118; Emmanuel Dunand, 140; Frances Brown, 12, 20, 23, 27, 30, 54, 59, 127, 144, 148; Gary Woods, London, 18, 29, 56, 60, 62, 66, 78, 91, 96, 99, 142; Mark Edwards, 112; Michael Collopy, 6, 9, 17, 32, 34, 46, 53, 69, 84, 88, 94, 100, 104, 116, 120, 121, 122, 130, 132, 137, 139, 147, 150; Polak Matthew, cover; Raghu Rai, 48; Syndication International, 50; Topham Picturepoint, 42, 73, 134; Zefa, 7.